NEW YORK GIANTS · SUPER BOWL CHAMPIONS

# XXI, JANUARY 25, 1987
## 39-20 VERSUS DENVER BRONCOS

# XXV, JANUARY 27, 1991
## 20-19 VERSUS BUFFALO BILLS

# XLII, FEBRUARY 3, 2008
## 17-14 VERSUS NEW ENGLAND PATRIOTS

# SUPER BOWL CHAMPIONS

## NEW YORK GIANTS

AARON FRISCH

CREATIVE EDUCATION

COVER: QUARTERBACK ELI MANNING

PAGE 2: RUNNING BACK TIKI BARBER CARRYING THE BALL

RIGHT: QUARTERBACK PHIL SIMMS THROWING A PASS

Published by Creative Education
P.O. Box 227, Mankato, Minnesota 56002
Creative Education is an imprint of The Creative Company
www.thecreativecompany.us

Book and cover design by Blue Design (www.bluedes.com)
Art direction by Rita Marshall
Printed by Corporate Graphics in the United States of
America

Photographs by Corbis (Bettmann), Dreamstime (Rosco),
Getty Images (Bill Cummings/NFL, Focus on Sport, Larry
French, Tom Hauck, Ben Liebenberg/NFL Photos, Al
Messerschmidt/NFL, Donald Miralle, NFL Photos, Robert
Riger, Jamie Squire, Damian Strohmeyer/Sports Illustrated,
Michael S. Yamashita)

Library of Congress Cataloging-in-Publication Data

Frisch, Aaron.
New York Giants / by Aaron Frisch.
p. cm. — (Super Bowl champions)
Includes index.
Summary: An elementary look at the New York Giants
professional football team, including its formation in 1925,
most memorable players, Super Bowl championships, and
stars of today.
ISBN 978-1-60818-023-3
1. New York Giants (Football team)—History—Juvenile
literature. I. Title. II. Series.

GV956.N4F75 2011
796.33'264097471—dc22          2010001020

CPSIA: 040110 PO1141

First Edition
9 8 7 6 5 4 3 2 1

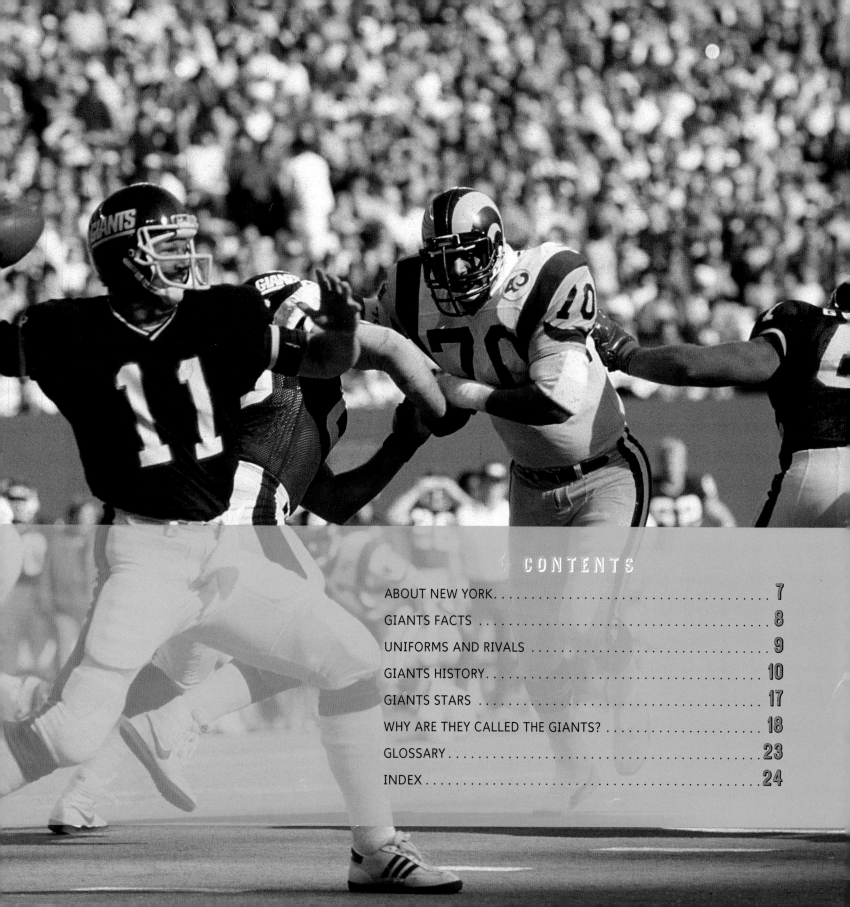

# CONTENTS

SUPER BOWL CHAMPIONS

New York is a city in the state of New York. It is the biggest city in America. About eight million people live there. The New York City area has a **stadium** called New Meadowlands Stadium that is the home of a football team called the Giants.

... NEW YORK CITY IS THE HOME OF MANY MAJOR SPORTS TEAMS ...

7

## GIANTS FACTS

First season:

**1925**

Conference/division:

**National Football Conference, East Division**

Super Bowl championships:

**XXI, January 25, 1987 / 39-20 versus Denver Broncos**
**XXV, January 27, 1991 / 20-19 versus Buffalo Bills**
**XLII, February 3, 2008 / 17-14 versus New England**
**Patriots**

Training camp location:

**Albany, New York**

NFL Web site for kids:

**http://nflrush.com**

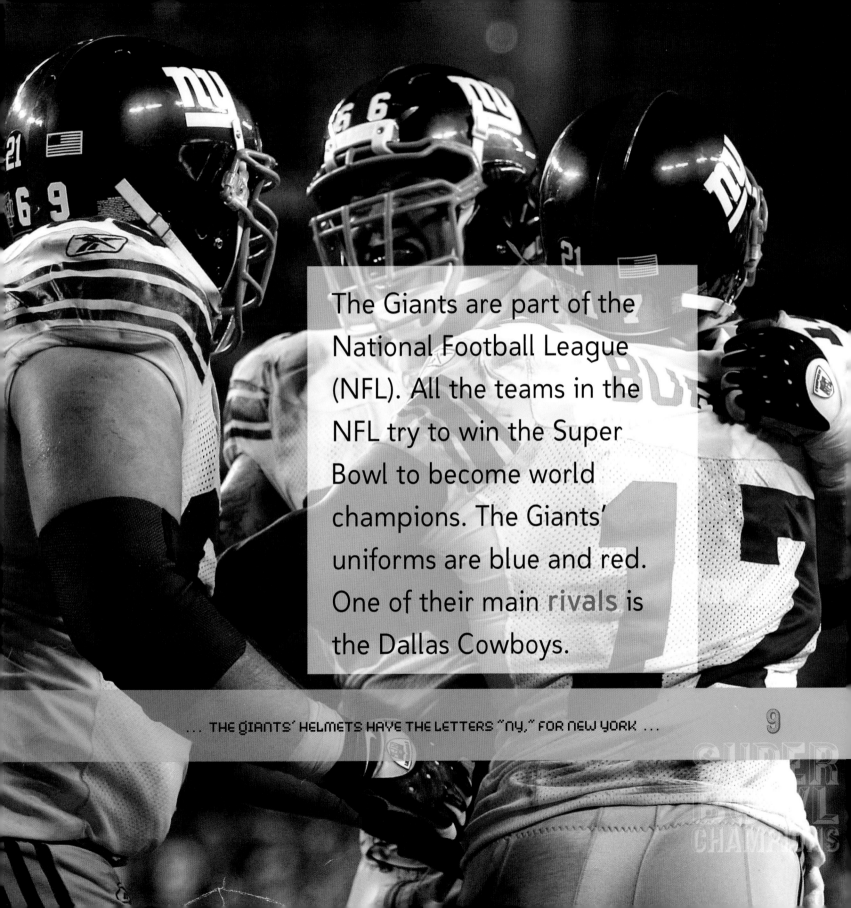

The Giants are part of the National Football League (NFL). All the teams in the NFL try to win the Super Bowl to become world champions. The Giants' uniforms are blue and red. One of their main **rivals** is the Dallas Cowboys.

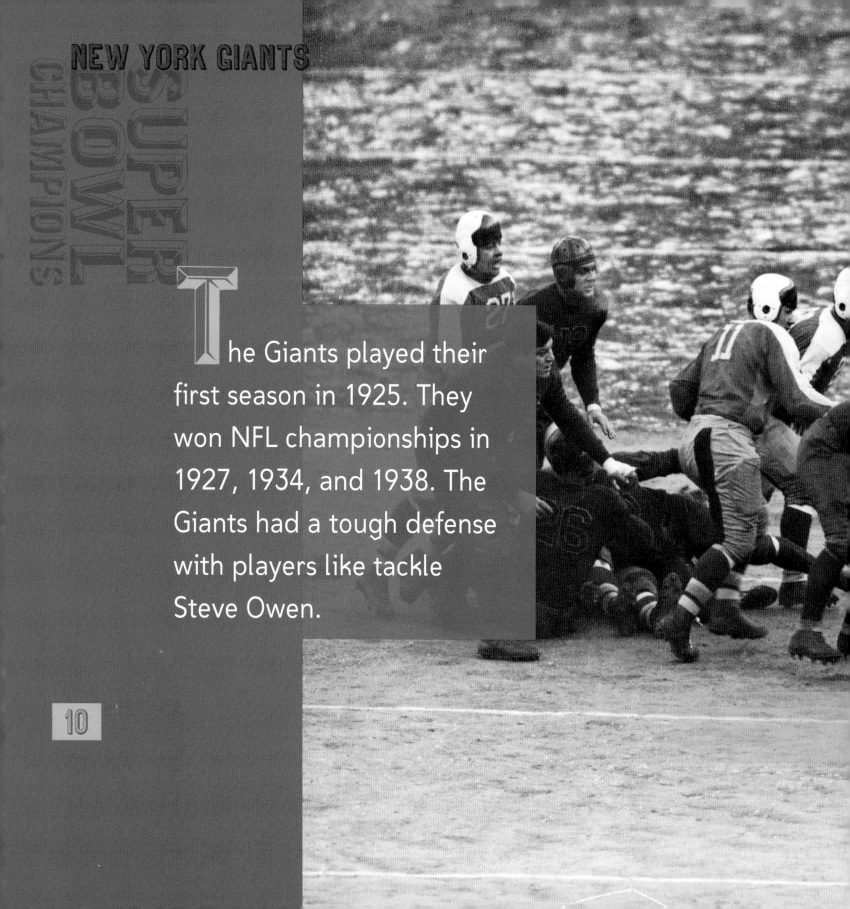

SUPER BOWL CHAMPIONS

The Giants played their first season in 1925. They won NFL championships in 1927, 1934, and 1938. The Giants had a tough defense with players like tackle Steve Owen.

... THE GIANTS BEAT THE CHICAGO BEARS FOR THE 1934 CHAMPIONSHIP ...

11

Say It Like This

Conerly:

*CAHN-er-lee*

In the 1950s, the Giants got a tough quarterback named Charlie Conerly. New York won another championship in 1956. The Giants got to the **playoffs** many times after that, but they lost every time.

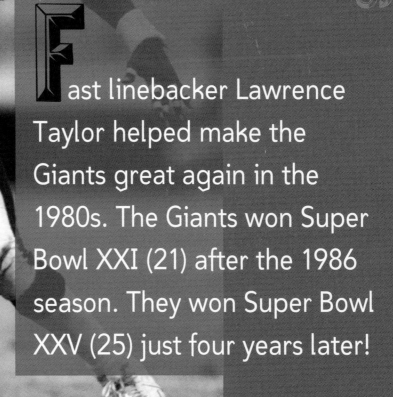

SUPER BOWL CHAMPIONS

Fast linebacker Lawrence Taylor helped make the Giants great again in the 1980s. The Giants won Super Bowl XXI (21) after the 1986 season. They won Super Bowl XXV (25) just four years later!

... CHARLIE CONERLY (LEFT) AND LAWRENCE TAYLOR (RIGHT) ...

... THE GIANTS WON SUPER BOWL XLII BY THREE POINTS ...

SUPER BOWL CHAMPIONS

The Giants won another championship after the 2007 season. New quarterback Eli Manning threw two touchdown passes to help beat the **undefeated** New England Patriots in Super Bowl XLII (42).

15

The Giants have had many stars. Mel Hein played in the 1930s. He was so good that he played both center and linebacker. Frank Gifford was a fast running back who scored more touchdowns than any other Giants player.

... MEL HEIN (LEFT) AND FRANK GIFFORD (RIGHT) ...

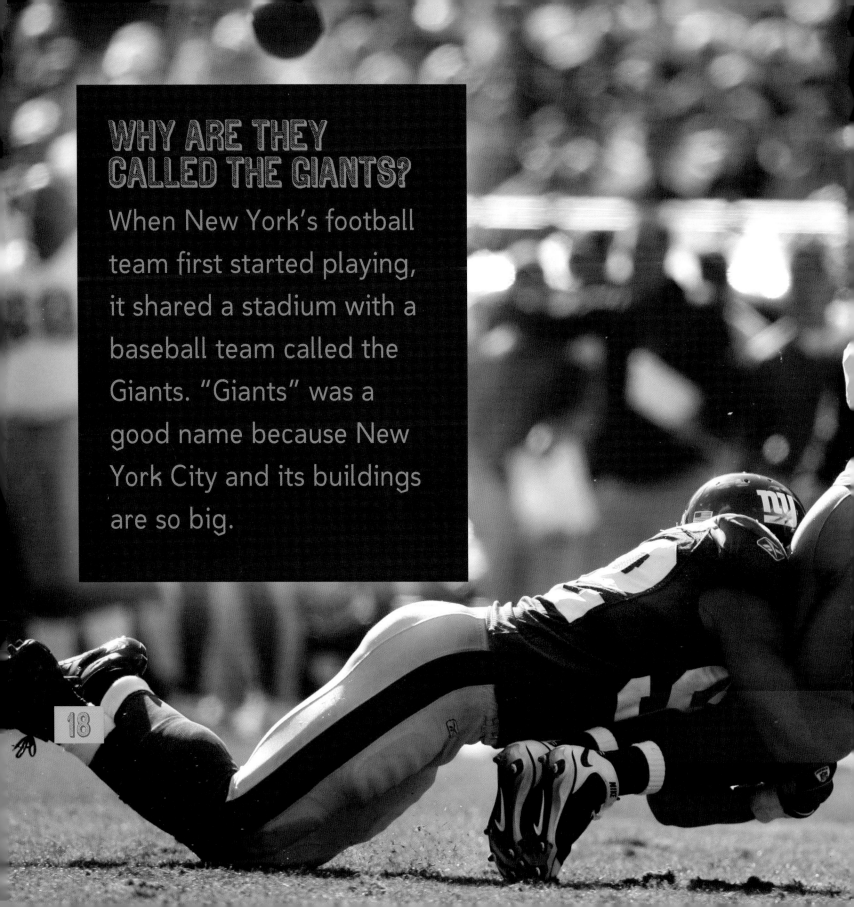

## WHY ARE THEY CALLED THE GIANTS?

When New York's football team first started playing, it shared a stadium with a baseball team called the Giants. "Giants" was a good name because New York City and its buildings are so big.

18

Say It Like This

Strahan:

**STRAY-han**

Quarterback Phil Simms
joined the Giants in 1979.
He led New York's offense
for 14 years. Defensive end
Michael Strahan was another
Giants star. In 2001, he set an
NFL **record** by making 22.5
quarterback **sacks**.

... MICHAEL STRAHAN PLAYED ALL OF HIS NFL SEASONS IN NEW YORK ...

19

... OSI UMENYIORA WAS HARD TO STOP WHEN HE CHASED QUARTERBACKS ...

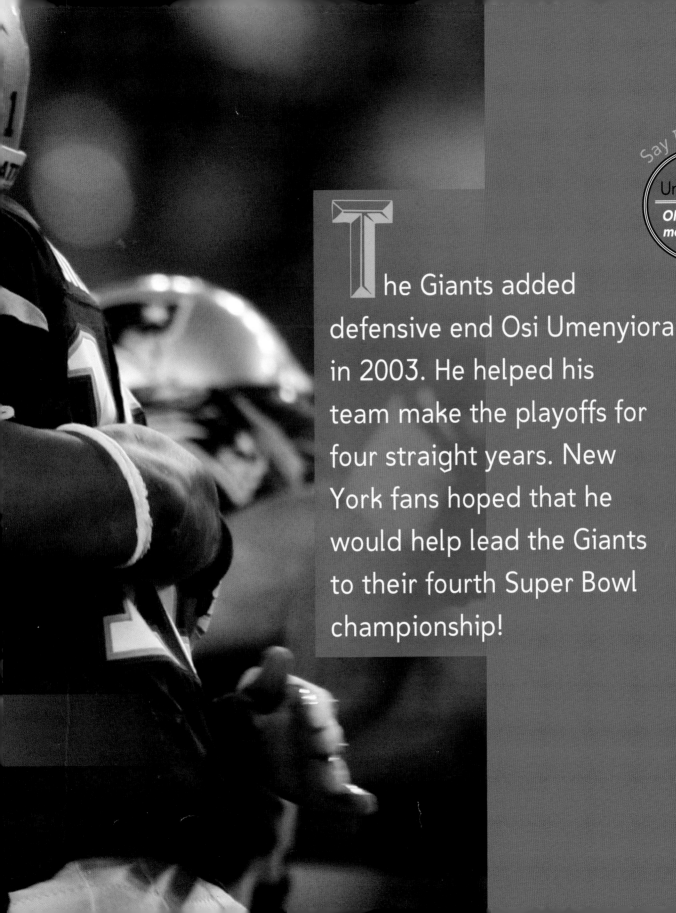

The Giants added defensive end Osi Umenyiora in 2003. He helped his team make the playoffs for four straight years. New York fans hoped that he would help lead the Giants to their fourth Super Bowl championship!

21
SUPER
BOWL
CHAMPIONS

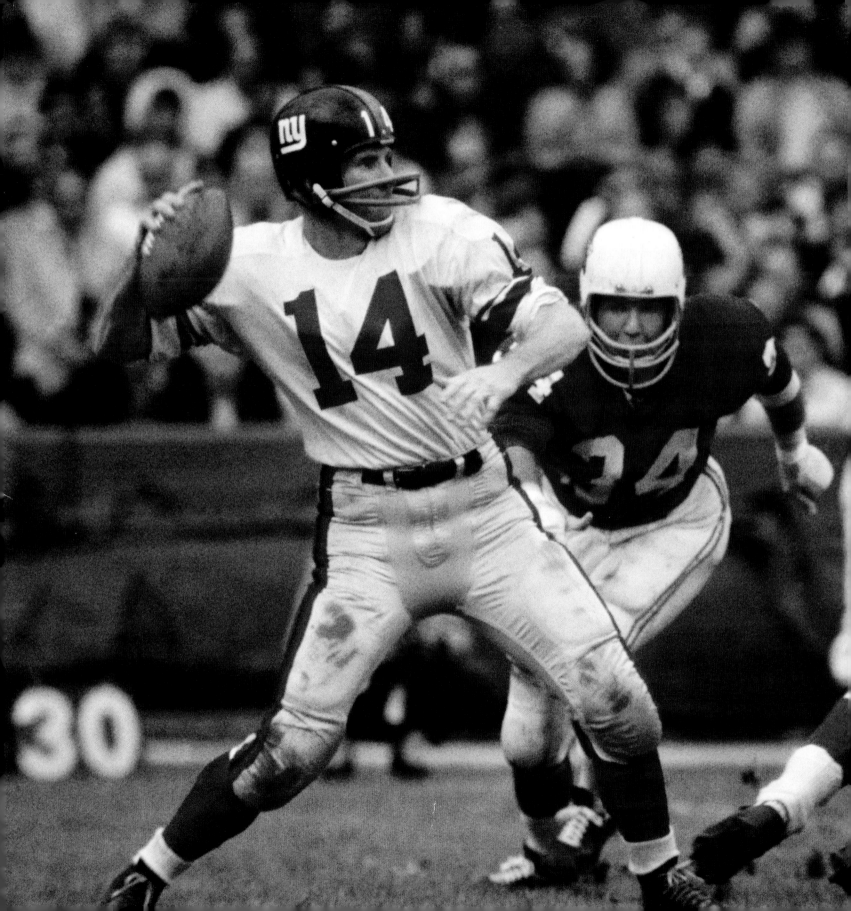

SUPER BOWL CHAMPIONS

# GLOSSARY

playoffs — games that the best teams play after a season to see who the champion will be

record — something that is the best or most ever

rivals — teams that play extra hard against each other

sacks — plays where a player tackles a quarterback who is trying to throw a pass

stadium — a large building that has a sports field and many seats for fans

undefeated — did not lose any games

24

# INDEX